THREE DIMENSIONAL SHAPES

CYLINDERS

Luana K. Mitten

Rourke

Publishing LLC
Vero Beach, Florida 32964

www.rourkepublishing.com

PHOTO CREDITS: © Raffaelo: page 7 top; © Eli Mordechai: page 7 bottom, 9; © Kun Jiang: page 15 top; © Pavel Siamionau: page 15 bottom; © Floortje: page 19 top, 21; © Sandra Nicol: page 19 bottom; © Klaudia Steiner: page 22 right; © akaplummer: page 23 right; © parema: page 23 left;

Editor: Kelli Hicks

Cover design by Nicola Stratford, bdpublishing.com

Interior Design by Heather Botto

Library of Congress Cataloging-in-Publication Data

Mitten, Luana K.
  Three dimensional shapes : cylinders / Luana K. Mitten.
     p. cm. -- (Concepts)
  ISBN 978-1-60472-416-5
  1. Cylinder (Mathematics)--Juvenile literature. 2. Shapes--Juvenile literature. 3. Geometry, Solid--Juvenile literature. I. Title. II. Title: Cylinders.
  QA491.M5695 2009
  516'.156--dc22
                                      2008018804

Printed in the USA

CG/CG

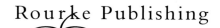

Rourke Publishing

www.rourkepublishing.com – rourke@rourkepublishing.com
Post Office Box 3328, Vero Beach, FL 32964

What makes this a cylinder?

Two circles with a tube between, that makes this a cylinder!

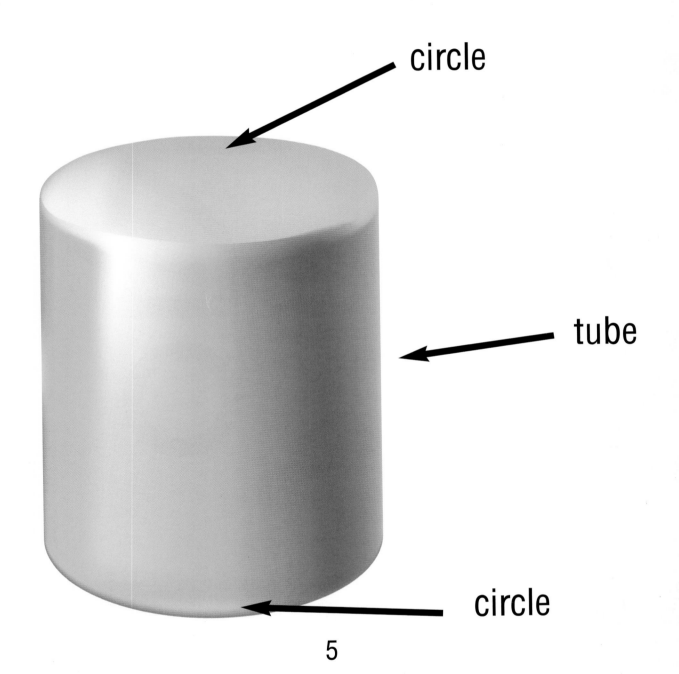

circle

tube

circle

5

Which can
is a cylinder?

6

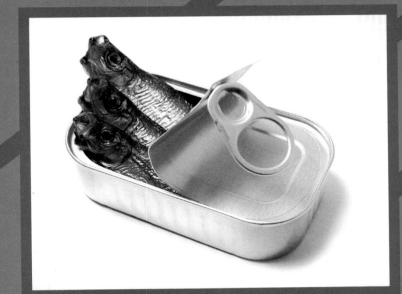

7

Two circles with a tube between, can of soup.

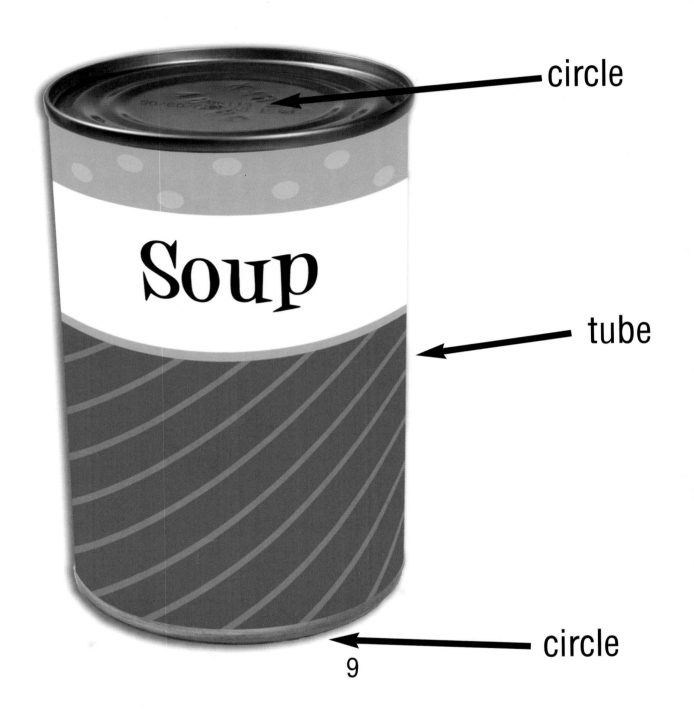

circle

tube

circle

9

Which box
is a cylinder?

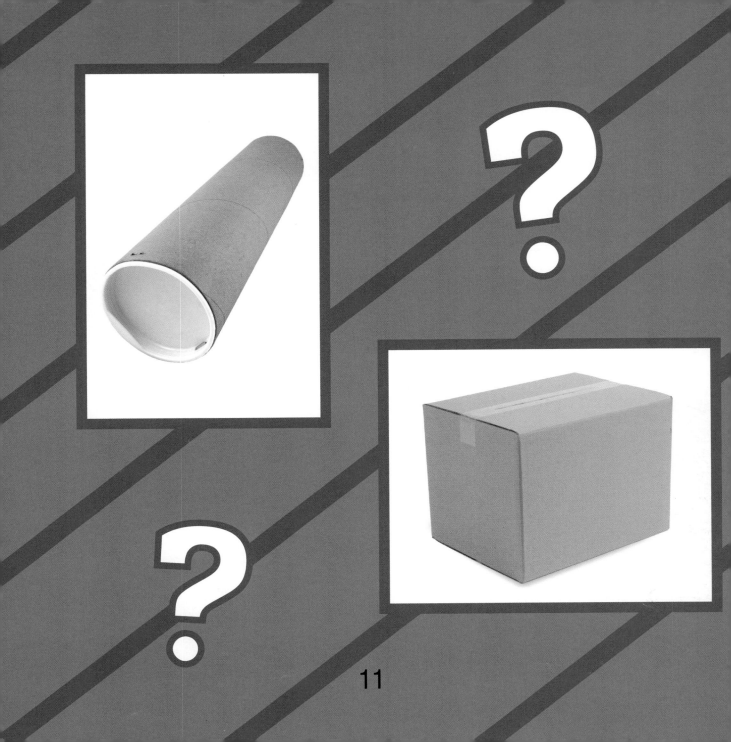

11

Two circles with a tube between, box for mailing.

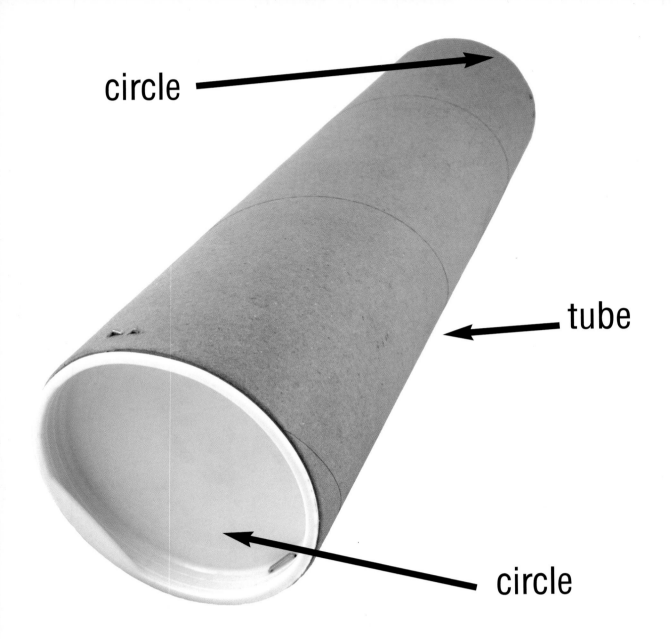

circle

tube

circle

13

Which blocks
are cylinders?

14

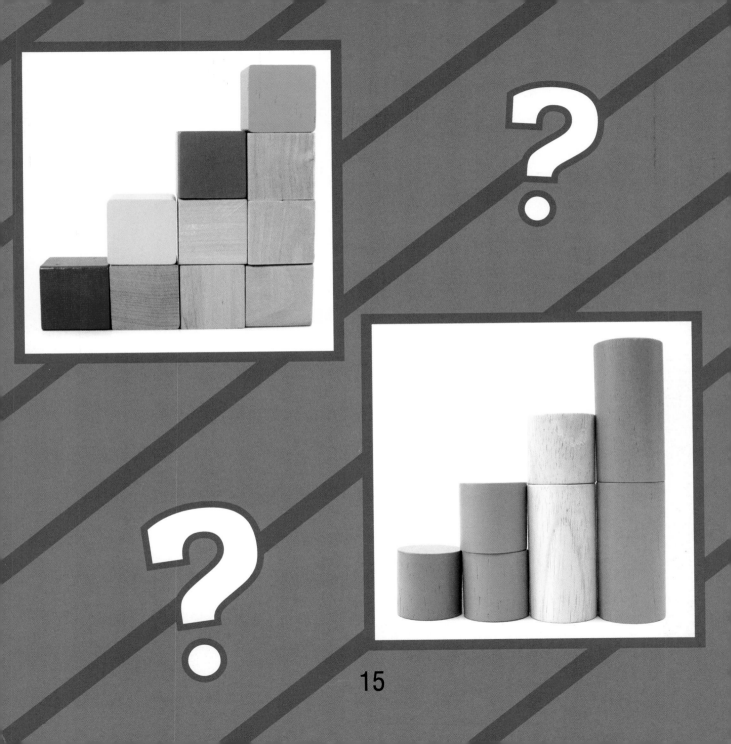

15

Two circles with a tube between, cylinder blocks.

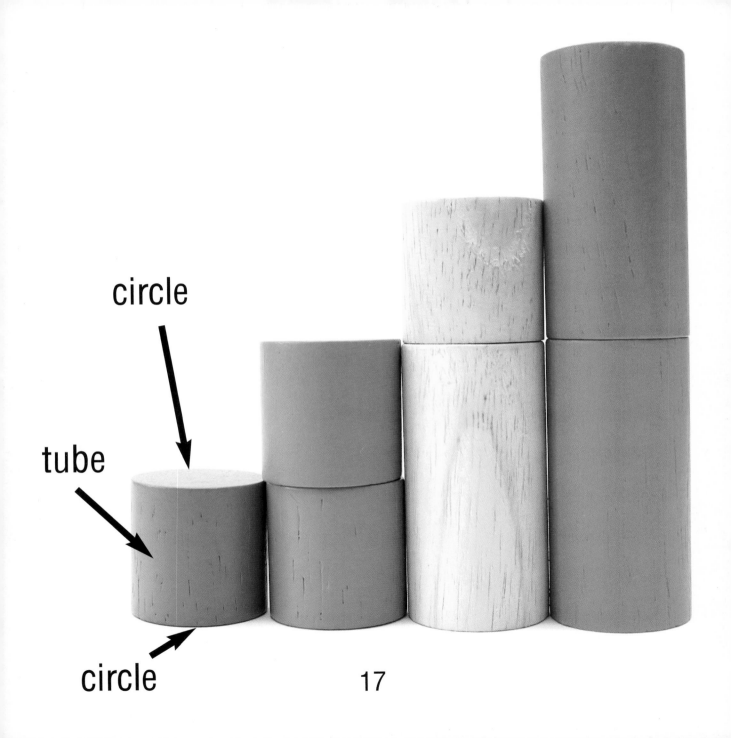

circle

tube

circle

17

Which candies
are cylinders?

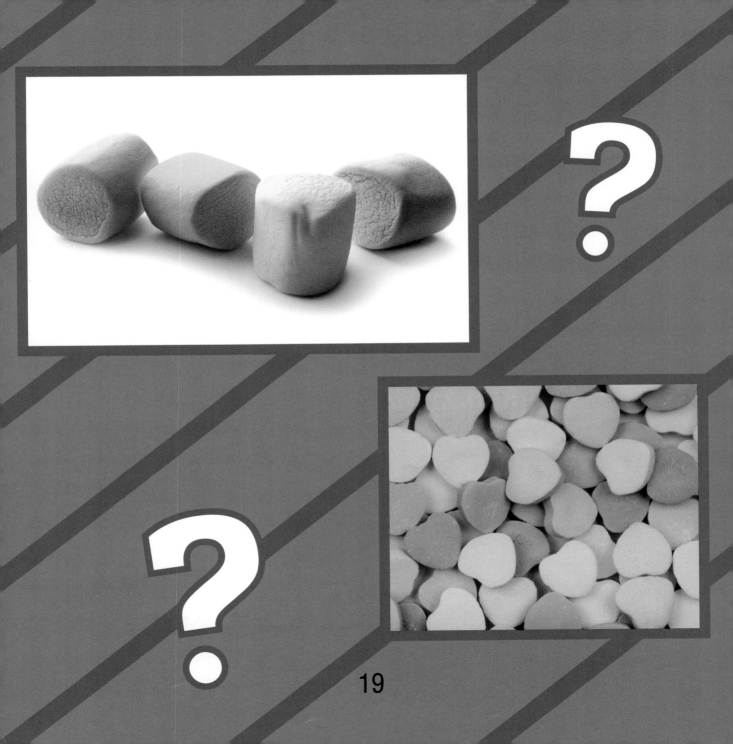

19

Two circles with a tube between, cylinder candies.

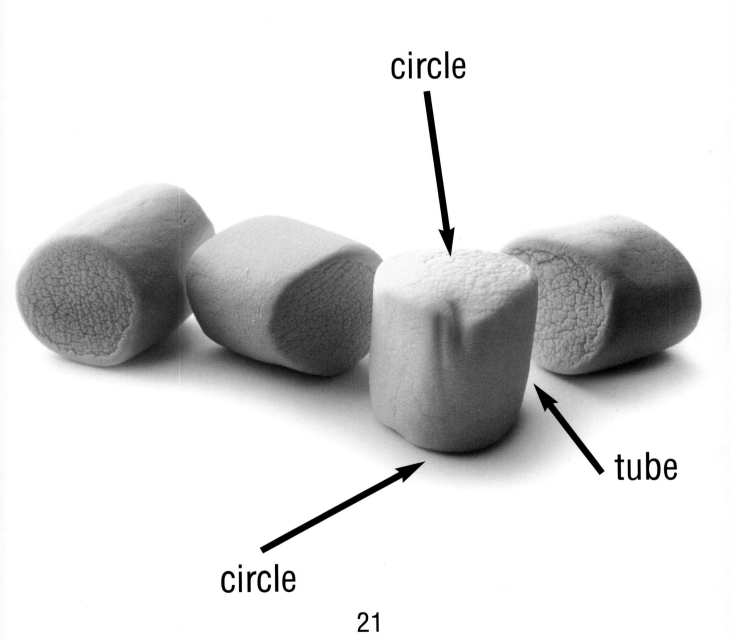

circle

circle

tube

21

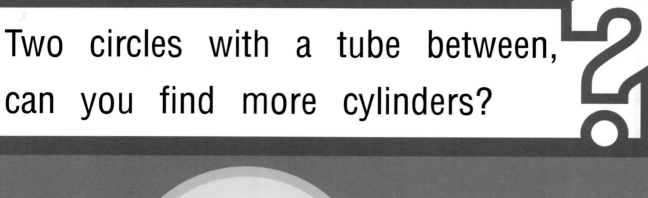

Two circles with a tube between, can you find more cylinders?

22

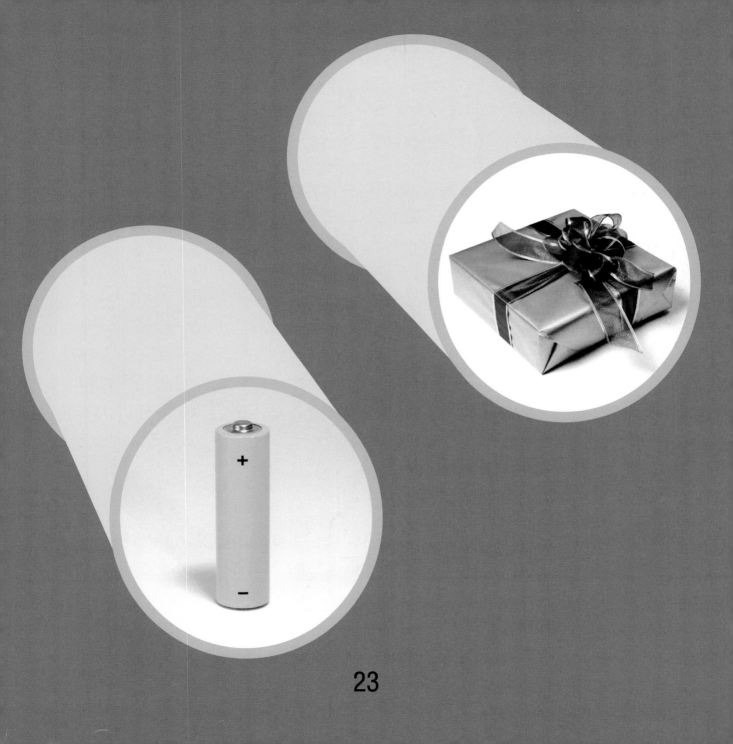

Index

blocks   14, 16
box   10, 12
can   6, 8, 12,
candies   18, 20
circles   4, 8, 12, 16, 20, 22

cylinder(s)   3, 4, 6, 10, 14, 16,
18, 20, 22
tube   4, 5, 8, 9, 12, 13, 16,
17, 20, 21, 22

Further Reading

Kalman, Bobbie. *What Shape is It?* Crabtree Publishing, 2007.
Senisi, Ellen B. *A 3-D Birthday Party*. Children's Press, 2006.

Recommended Websites

www.42explore.com/geomet.htm
www.atozkidsstuff.com/shpes.html
www.abc.net.au/countusin/default.htm

About the Author

Luana Mitten lives in Tampa, Florida with her family. Sipping fruit smoothies through a cylinder shaped straw is her favorite afternoon snack.

24